How to Analyze People Fast

Easily Read People Like an Open Book

By: Tammy Jones

Contents

How to Analyze People Fast 1

Easily Read People Like an Open Book 1

Introduction...4

Chapter 1-Read People with the Eye Technique........................7

-Step 1-Memorize a quick frame of the eyes 7

-Step 2- Decipher the Look..7

-Step 3-Draw your Conclusions 8

-Step 4- Record Your Conclusions...8

How to use this technique in your everyday life?......................9

Chapter 2-Analyze People Through Their Body Language......11

The arms movements 12

-What to retain from this chapter..16

Chapter 3-Analyze People Through Their Habits 17

-First, distinguish bad from good habits 18

-A good habit: A bad habit is a habit that has a negative impact on someone and in extension, the people around them. Good habits count unhealthy habits, excessive habits, and habits that bother others. Examples of bad and excessive habits are the ones linked to a compulsive excessive behavior like cleaning too much, being a control freak, having no limits when it comes to alcohol or food, etc. 18

-Understand the need for these habits of this person 18

-Note the key components of the habits that give you, in turn, the key components of this person's nature................................19

-What to retain from this chapter: 21

Chapter 4-Analyze People Through Their Words 22

Pay Attention to Certain Words...22

Pay attention to the body language that accompanies certain words or views. 24

Weight the choice of words to see if it can really reflect their nature...25

-What to retain from this chapter: 27

Conclusion 28

Introduction

I want to thank you and congratulate you for downloading the book, *"How to Analyze People Fast: Easily Read People Like an Open Book "*.

This book contains proven steps and strategies on how to easily read your peers and perhaps random people you meet in your everyday life.

Reading other people is important because it helps you deal with unpredictable behaviors from your peers and it also helps understand a lot of situations much faster. In other words, it helps you predict people's behaviors, but it also helps you decipher or read others who don't easily express themselves or the ones who have things to hide. Reading people is not just something you do for fun, in fact, reading people can help you protect yourself in your everyday life, as well as helping you foreseeing potential threats at work or with your relationships.

Thanks again for downloading this book, I hope you enjoy it!

Chapter 1-Read People with the Eye Technique

You've probably heard the expression that eyes, "the eyes are the windows to one's soul", which could be true. Think about it, we tend to learn a lot about someone's instant feelings by simply looking at them, and their eyes tell us if they are sad, concerned, angry, scared, etc. In other words, your eyes tell more about you than you can ever realize.

For those who are clueless about the eye reading technique, we will now explain how this technique works and how you can benefit off of it.

-Step 1-Memorize a quick frame of the eyes

One of the biggest mistakes people often make when having a conversation is to only focus on the words of the other person. We could save ourselves a lot of unnecessary emotional outbursts and misconceptions if we only focused on the other person's eyes. That's because a person's eyes give us a different vibe, which corresponds to their emotions at a given time. So, your first step here would be to memorize a frame image of the eyes of the other person, just like you would do if you were taking a regular picture of that person's eyes. Then, take 2 minutes focusing on that imagery (meaning that you have to focus on that frame in order to get used to it). Then, move on to the next step.

-Step 2- Decipher the Look

Your next step is quite simple, and it involves deciphering or interpreting the other person's look (referring to their eyes.) Here, you will actually label the frame. So, here if you think that the other person's eyes gave vibes of sadness, happiness, depressions, or anger this frame that you recorded in your mind should be labeled as sad, happy, depressed or angry. So, this step involves labeling the eye frame that you've just memorized on step 1.

-Step 3-Draw your Conclusions

The third step involves drawing your conclusions, where you must finalize your findings (the ones made on step 2), by playing the frame you've memorized on step 1 several times, the following way:

- Play the frames, one by one as if you were viewing sliding images (it should have a PowerPoint effect, where the image appears and disappears every 2 to 3 seconds just enough for you to see it and take note of it.)

- As each frame plays in front of you, you should describe them with your own words, meaning that if you visualize a frame of eyes that describe sadness, you should say, "These are sad eyes", for madness, "these eyes are mad eyes", etc.

- You must play the memorized frames at least 5 times in a row. This way you get accustomed to them easily. This will help train your eyes and mind by conditioning them to these frames.

These steps will help you identify a person's emotions with ease, help you chose your words wisely and also help you determine where you should stand when it comes to a certain relationship with someone.

-Step 4- Record Your Conclusions

The last step involves actually drawing these eyes expressions. This step is important because not only it helps you track record of what you observed (concerning how people's eyes change every time their emotions change), and it is also good for practice. You don't have to be good in drawing, but simply reproduce what you see when you look at someone's eyes while you are communicating with them.

How to use this technique in your everyday life?

So, in order for this technique to be effective, you'll have to know how to use it the right way (of course). In our previous sections we've shown you how to prepare for this technique, now we will show you how to use it.

First of all, know that your preparation phase counts steps 1, 2, 3, and 4, but in practice, only steps 1 and 2 will be covered. This is because we consider that for you to apply this technique you must first get used to reading emotions through someone's eyes and this can only be done after mastering steps 3 and 4.

So, in real life, all you have to do is take frames of someone's eyes, which will enable you to read/decipher emotions with ease in the end.

Let's now use an example to see how this technique works. Imagine that you own a small business and that you need to lay off an employee because this employee is not as effective as you wish he would. Now, you might get embarrassed to do so, and you don't really know what to say because you fear the other person might end up getting really mad at you. Now, here's your way out of it, by reading through this person's eyes and knowing just what to say or do.

-On the first phase, we figured that you'd ask this person to come into your office and have them to sit down. The first thing you will probably see is the concern in their eyes (that's the first frame you should take and memorize).

- On the second phase, this person looks concerned judging by their eyes, let's reassure them. Now, you can choose to reassure them by encouraging them to improve themselves. After your wordings, the person now feels relaxed.

- On the third phase, move on with the conversation and let them know what you've got in your mind, which is you wanting to fire them. The person may feel shocked, sad, or perhaps they would have expected it. At this very instant, take or memorize a frame of their eyes in order to read their emotions, so that you know what to do next. So, here, if they are upset you can decide to give them another chance, if they expected it, well you are 100% right to say what you are saying.

- On the fourth phase, finalize the discussion. Take/memorize their eye frame for one last time and whatever you are reading at this very instant will let you know what you have to say next or what you should do.

This technique as you could have seen it will help you socialize with people a bit better and it will also help you predict their behavior before they happen.

-What to retain from this chapter:

-Eyes have the ability to tell what a person really thinks or how they feel.

-Learning to decipher what one's eyes tell you might help you handle difficult situations in your life.

-Recording these emotions by drawing them might help you train better for the eye reading technique.

Chapter 2-Analyze People Through Their Body Language

Another technique that you've probably heard of is the one involving analyzing someone's body language. This may resemble the eye technique a little more because it also involves body parts, but it is a bit more complex. We judge this technique as being more complex because one cannot automatically predict how the body would react faced with a certain situation. That's why studying certain reflexes when faced with a certain situation are important here.

There are a few things you must take note here:

1- You can lead someone to reveal things about themselves by triggering one's body language.

2- You can also learn something from someone from afar, and that normally involves deep thoughts that are not always shared.

3- Body language counts movements that involve body parts that are attached to a muscle (which means most of your body). So, one's mouth, eyes, arms, fingers, feet, neck, and even and a combination of several body parts may be considered as body language.

4- You must also learn to distinguish between movements that are neutral and those who really translate into something. The key point to remember here is that very few people can stay neutral in most situations, whether they are chaotic or ones where you should rejoice (it's also called having self-control), and the other thing is that most people will forcibly have a reaction once faced with a situation and each gesture means something.

Let's now go through a series of hand gesture that you should know about in order to better read people.

The hand gestures

People using hand gestures during conversations often do so as a sign of comfort (where they want to show to the other person or persons, they are talking to that they are comfortable talking about a certain subject, possibly because they master this subject.) It can also be a way to protect themselves when they are misunderstood, or they feel threatened. The hands are always brought forward, where the person would play with one, two, or several fingers at a time (you often see politicians use their hands and fingers most of the time when speaking to their audience, which makes them very convincible and presentable at the same time.)

On the other hand, when someone feels threatened, they tend to put their hands forward, fingers spread or not spread as a sign that the situation needs to simmer down, and that they are ready to negotiate.

So, overall, here hands gesture must be read as:

- A sign of comfort or confidence during a conversation.

- An attempt to calm a bowling situation down.

The arms movements

With arm movements, things seem to be less peaceful and less civilized than with hand gestures. Most of the time, people use their arms when they are unable to hold their emotions in. In a few instances, it can also express an outburst of uncontrollable emotions like an outburst of joy, for instance. So, if for instance, you see someone speaking loudly and making abrupt arm movements it means that this person is very angry and that you should try and calm the situation down instead of making it worse. The same thing goes for joy, where, for instance, during a football match we would raise our hands up, showing how extremely happy we are after a goal has been scored.

So, here arms movements should be read as:

- A sign that the person is boiling with anger inside.

- A sign that the person is extremely happy and can't control their emotions.

The facial expressions

The facial expressions have to do with the movements one makes with their mouths, eyes, and sometimes a combination of several parts of your face. Facial expressions are the easiest to read because most people have the same ones and for another obvious reason, they are very visible and easy to memorize. The thing about facial expressions is that they are often used to replace a group of words, and that's why they should be taken seriously most of the time. So, to sum it up let's summarize what some of the most common facial expressions are:

- When someone stretches their eyes, it's a sign of disbelief of something they've just witnessed or heard.

- When someone tightens their eyes with a slight backward movement of the neck, it means that they doubt what you are saying.

- When someone stretches all their mouth muscles on one corner of their mouth or again, if they tighten them in order to give an elongated shape to your mouth it means that they are disappointed.

- When someone suddenly looks down after hearing something it means that they are disappointed.

- When someone looks up, they are either boiling with some intense emotions or just annoyed.

The feet/legs movements

Someone's feet movements can also help you learn about what they are thinking. Feet or leg movements are easy to read because they normally translate into a state of nervousness. The person is either bothered by something or growing impatient. The typical legs and feet movements are the following:

- Knees being brought together back and forth, which is a sign of impatience.

- One Leg flexed while on the seating position, moving left and right, which is either a sign of nervousness or impatience.

- Tapping your foot on the floor, which is also a sign of nervousness from the person.

The combination movements

Combination movements are movements that regroup hand, legs, and sometimes facial movements. They have nothing in particular because they, overall, mean the same thing as the ones we've already explained earlier.

Here are a few examples:

- If you see someone flexing their mouth muscles in order to elongate the lips forward and bringing their legs, or one leg left and right, it means that the person is impatient or annoyed.

- When a person claps their hands and taps on their feet at the same time while moving forward or back and forth, it means that the person wants your attention as they are growing impatient.

- When someone bends their head to one side while they are talking to you, it means that they are not taking you seriously. If they are using their hands while talking it means that even though they don't take you seriously, they still want to find a common goal with you.

- When people put their hands on their chick it's either a false or neutral sign because they are simply tired, or, again, they are bored to be around you.

- When someone puts their hands on top of their chin, it's a sign that they are very confident and serene with their opinions.

- When someone puts their hands behind their back it's a sign of submission in a way that they want you to consider them as one of yours.

- If the person puts their hands (by joining them together) in front of them it's a sign of superiority and an attempt to control the situation.

- When someone puts their hands on their waist it's a sign of dominance, where they expect results from the other person.

Let's use an example to see how this reading technique can help you. Imagine that you find someone in an argument with someone else, and this person ends the conversation, not saying anything but stretching their eye muscles by stretching their eyes. Now, before you say anything to this person, it would be best for you to decipher their body language. Now with reference to our section about facial expressions, stretching your eyes, here means that you are in disbelief with what you've just heard, which might make you upset and in a bad mood for the rest of the day. So, for your own sake here, after reading this body language, you should, perhaps wait till the next day before you decide to address this person.

So, here, body language helps you with understanding what the person feels without them having to say anything, and you also get to know what to say and what not to say to that person for your own sake.

-What to retain from this chapter

- Body language helps you improve your relationship with people.

- Body language involves most of your body parts.

- It is important to know about body language because sometimes they replace words more effectively.

Chapter 3-Analyze People Through Their Habits

If there's a way to read people effectively, it's through their habits. In other words, once you know what people like, how they organize themselves, and also what they fear it is very easy to study them and even further, predict their thoughts and movements. One reason why you should learn to read people through their habits is that people hate bad surprises. This means that people should think of facing life prepared and ready to fight constraints as much as they can. So, how is it that habits easily reflect someone's nature? The reasons are very simple, and we've numbered a few of them below:

- Habits can tell you who you are because they are often linked to your goals.

- The way you organize yourself can reveal how structured and sane you are.

- Sane habits can tell if you have a long-term vision of your life that is geared towards self-improvement (you can also detect if the person is self-sufficient, has high or low self-esteem, etc.)

- Habits can also tell if you are trustworthy because someone who makes sure they take care of themselves will tend to recreate this behavior at work or with other's projects.

Added to this, you also have to face the fact that habits, whether they are good or bad, can also reveal a chain of characteristics that can be very useful for you. So, how do you read someone through their habits, or if you prefer, what should you look for when it comes to reading someone's habit?

-First, distinguish bad from good habits

People have to distinguish between the two so that they don't confuse them since the goal of being able to read someone is to be able to benefit from their good side and not inherit any of their flaws. So, here are definitions of a good habit and a bad habit:

-A bad habit: A good habit is one that has a positive impact on a person, and on others in extension. Examples of good habits are waking up early, going to bed late, spacing your meals, asking for permission, saying thank you after receiving something, etc.

-A good habit: A bad habit is a habit that has a negative impact on someone and in extension, the people around them. Good habits count unhealthy habits, excessive habits, and habits that bother others. Examples of bad and excessive habits are the ones linked to a compulsive excessive behavior like cleaning too much, being a control freak, having no limits when it comes to alcohol or food, etc.

-Understand the need for these habits of this person

After you understand the difference between a good habit and a bad one, you should now understand why they are in a person's life so that you can better read that person. So, here's a list of clues you should consider once you've noted a certain habit with someone:

- Habits are often linked to a person's childhood experience, good or bad it might be very difficult for them to detach themselves from them.

- Habits are often put in place in order for people to take control of their lives.

- There is a difference between inherited habits and habits that we acquire later on in life.

- Acquired habits often demonstrate a person's strength in character, while habits that are often kept from childhood to adulthood demonstrate that a person might keep some very conservative views while they evolve in life, or that they are also not keen to change.

- Habits, in essence, give a sense of balance to a person. You have to draw the difference between a healthy balance and a non-healthy one (you can refer yourself to the definition we gave about good and bad habits earlier.)

By understanding why these habits are in a person's life, you will be able to draw some conclusions that will help you better position yourself when it comes to your relationship with this person.

-Note the key components of the habits that give you, in turn, the key components of this person's nature

After drawing a link between a habit, the reason why it is there in the first place you can now start reading this person, in other words, you will now be able to read this person effectively. This is the most technical part of this technique which wants you to identify a habit, draw a few key components of these habits and then draw your own conclusions. We will now use a few examples to show you how you can proceed here.

-Example 1: Person's habit= The person Likes waking up early:

- Key components of the habit: Ready before everyone else, able to accomplish more, more energy than others.

- What is most likely to be this person's nature: Hard worker, organized, focused.

-Example 2: Person's habit= The person likes to have items of a certain color around them:

- Key components of this person's habit: Defines their mood and purpose through a color.

- What is most likely to be this person's nature: Very limited, very refined, very complicated.

-Example 3: Person's habit=The person likes washing their hands all the time:

- Key components of this person's habit: Very knit, obsessed with being clean, probably not enthusiastic about being around large crowds of people.

- What is most likely to be this person's nature: Very organized, pays attention to details, paranoid, very controlling.

-Example 4: The person only dates people who look a certain way:

- Key components of this person's habit: Has preferences, is sensitive to certain details, is difficult to please.

- What is most likely to be this person's nature: is prone to fetishism, closed-minded, stubborn, is very specific into what they want in life and what they expect from others.

-Example 5: The person likes resisting orders:

- Key components of this person's habit: Can be lazy, determined.

- What is most likely to be this person's nature: Independent, rebellious, engaged when they decide to, libertarian and a free-spirited.

Note that although you can learn to read people through their habits, there would be times where you are able to read just a little bit of this person's character, and at the same time, you can read them to perfection. This is not to say that the technique is not effective or doesn't help you to be right all the time, like a mathematical rule would do, but it's just that it is dealing with human nature and human nature seems to be very versatile sometimes.

You should try to apply the guidelines we've given you throughout this chapter and train yourself in reading others. This technique like all the other ones can help you maintain better relationships with others and also help you predict others' thoughts and movements.

-What to retain from this chapter:

- Habits are often shaped according to someone's character.

- Habits are either good or bad and both should be taken into consideration when you wish to read someone.

-Taking note of the key components surrounding someone's habits can help you have an idea about this person's true nature.

- Habits can either give you a partial idea of the person, but they can also give you all the details about this person.

- Human nature is very versatile, which means that one's habits can't always reveal everything about someone.

Chapter 4-Analyze People Through Their Words

Words can tell a lot about people and that's because they have been thought before being told and also, the thoughts we share with others are the products of our beliefs and experience. In other words, words are, most of the time, very personal. Overall, words can give you details about the following: One's emotions, one's fears, one's nature, one's knowledge, and everything you can think of that can help you learn about someone as soon as they open their mouth.

Most people wonder if there are key words that one should pay attention to or if the best way to do this is to listen to the person's story and then draw your own conclusions. The answer is that the person who wishes to read a person through their words should:

1- Pay attention to certain words

2- Pay attention to the body language that accompanies certain words or views.

3- Weight the choice of words to see if it can really reflect their nature.

We will now explain each one of these points below, in more details.

Pay Attention to Certain Words

As said earlier, words can reveal a lot about someone's nature. You have to note that it's not about a specific word, but how you formulate what you think (your point of view). This way, you are able to weight someone's scope of certain things and know more about their nature. But amongst these words that we all say sometimes, there are some that are very revealing. This is because when we express ourselves there's always an intention behind our words. And these intentions are most of the time:

- The intention to convince with words like, "Do you get it?", or "do you get what I'm trying to say?"

- The intention to get away with something with words like, "I don't know what you are talking about", "I don't get it".

- The intention to deceive with words like, "you can trust me with your life"

- The intention to obtain some kind of compassion with words like, "I am begging you please", "please give me a chance."

- The intention to obtain some acknowledgment with words like, "Look at me", "listen to me", "I need your intentions".

Added to these types of words you have other elements that you should take into consideration:

- The person's tone. Tone, like body language earlier, also helps read emotions through the voice. It gives a tempo or, if you prefer, a temperature to the words so that you know if the person you are talking to feels aggravated when they speak or if they are calm.

- Once again, the person's body language. The body language helps further decipher someone's intention while the person is talking. For instance, it is easy to tell if someone is lying or trying to get away from you because while they talk to you, they are also acting a certain way.

So, once you've paid attention to words that supposedly describe an intention make sure you also pay attention to the person's tone and their body language. This is mostly because the tone and body language make part of your way of communicating, in other words, your tone and body language play the same role as words.

Pay attention to the body language that accompanies certain words or views.

We would like to stress more on a person's body language because sometimes they reveal more than words themselves. This mostly happens when something unexpected happens and we have to look for words in the following contexts (there could be more):

- We need to justify ourselves.

- We need to lie.

- We need to escape an embarrassing situation.

- We need to avoid answering questions.

So, overall, we may find the right wording to help us achieve these situations, but our body language will always reveal the truth. Here are examples of movements or body languages that follow the four situations quoted above:

- We say things that help us find a justification for a certain behavior but our body language shows otherwise because we avoid looking at the other person in the eye. What does it mean? That we want to impose our view even though the other person in front of us is right. We are just not going to let them get away with a victory over us.

- We say something because we are in a deep need to lie. Our body language says otherwise because we are trying to cut the conversation short, so we adopt an unpredictable behavior by making jokes or being unexpectedly jovial over nothing. This means that we are trying to get away with a lie and also trying to cover our intention as fast as we can.

- We say something because we need to escape an embarrassing situation. Our body language shows that we are actually embarrassed because not only do we sweat, but we also blow and puff uncontrollably asking the other person why it is so hot all of the sudden. The body language is trying to tell everybody watching you at this moment that you are embarrassed and ashamed of the situation, even if you say otherwise.

- We say something because we need to avoid answering certain questions, but our body language says that we are withholding something because we, all of the sudden, find something to do like, for instance, pretending to clean the house in the middle of the night.

So, take note of people's body language to really know what is going on. This way you know what to do or what to say to them at the right time.

Weight the choice of words to see if it can really reflect their nature.

Another and final way to know the true meaning of words would be to try and weigh words as they come out of the other person's mouth. But this technique only works for simple words, like yes or no, common expressions, and often with small/brief answers and not long conversations. Here, you would have to pay attention to the following:

- The tone of the person's voice.

- The timing, which has to do with the time it takes them to answer.

- And again, the body language.

Let's use an example to illustrate this technique a bit further.

Imagine that you've noticed that your lover was a bit too secretive lately. She talks on the phone more frequently, refuses to have any sort of intimacy with you. You suspect that she might be unfaithful, but you might be wrong. So, you decided to investigate by trying to read her. So, in order to be methodical, you will have to look for the following:

- The intention behind her words (what does she truly mean?)

- Her body language (is she trying to avoid locking eyes with you? Is she pretending to be busy while you are talking to her?)

- The tone behind her voice (can you sense behind her tone that she is not being truthful?)

- The timing it takes her to answer simple questions (how long does it take her to answer a question?)

And also ask yourself:

- If she's trying to justify herself a bit too much.

- If she is trying to lie.

- If she is embarrassed and tries to escape the situation.

- And if the person tries to avoid your questions.

Once you are able to answer all these questions, you can now draw your own conclusions. Meaning that:

- If this person avoids your questions, it's that they have something to hide.

- If this person is lying to you then maybe they are taking you for granted.

- If this person justifies themselves a bit too much it should be read as a way for her to conceal the truth as much as possible.

- If this person is embarrassed it should be read as them proving your suspicions right.

Overall, wordings and everything that serves into having a conversation (tone, body language, the timing you choose to speak or formulate words) can help you read into someone a bit better. Like with other techniques learning to read someone can help you decipher what the other person refuses to clearly divulge and also helps you predict the other person's actions.

-What to retain from this chapter:
- Words can also help you read about people

- You also have to pay attention to someone's body language, because they will tell you more than words do.

- Tone and timing should also be considered when analyzing someone's words.

Conclusion

Thank you again for downloading this book!

I hope this book was able to help you have a clearer idea about the things you should really look at when you want to read someone. It is important because sometimes, words alone, and people's testimony are not enough to reveal their true nature or intentions. Reading people by looking at things like their habits, facial expressions, and body language gives you an advantage and help you keep the upper hand in most situations.

The next step is to start reading others by doing the following:

- Learning to read people expressions and knowing what they truly mean.

- Learning to decipher all kinds of body languages and better position yourself when it comes to your relationship with others.

- Learning to pay attention to people's habits to know who they really are.

- And finally, learning to read through people's words.

Overall, learn to read people and become better at predicting others quickly.

Finally, if you enjoyed this book, then I'd like to ask you for a favor, would you be kind enough to leave a review for this book on Amazon? It'd be greatly appreciated!

Thank you and good luck!

9 781797 925028